THANK THE SWEET WATERS

Creative Director: Saeah Wood
Editorial Director: Amy Reed
Editorial: Tiana Reynolds
Design: Ivica Jandrijević
Cover Illustration: Elizabeth Evey
Author Photo: Helen Joy

Grateful acknowledgment to Jessica Jacobs for the use of her lines "Don't ever think it didn't matter" and "Plainly said, I needed the kind of love" in the poem "Villanelle for When We End."

Library of Congress Control Number: 2025915577

Paperback ISBN: 978-1-955671-86-6
E-book ISBN: 978-1-955671-87-3

otterpine.com
Asheville, NC

Thank the Sweet Waters

BY

LUCILLE MAY

OTTERPINE

To Morgan,

who always wants the first draft.

And to Simon,

who said yes.

Table of Contents

I. Falling in Love Together

II. Love in Practice

III. What Matters

I.

Falling in Love Together

This Is a Love Poem

I want you to be happy
clumsily, simply
the color of the sky
sun-striped
rain-wet
mild, each breath
the color is happy
no matter the shade
or wind gauge
and I underneath, gazing at the expanse
my mind pressed against your art
like a chest I could feel the heart in
words unwrapped and passed
playthings, courting gifts, condolence flowers
replacements
for another life
just
as heart-mashing
as this one.

The First Few Dates

At first, there is heat that heaves up water
and soaks the air. It loosens movement
and the sweat across your lightning skin gathers.
You can feel each hot and heavy moment.

It's generating a wet vitality—
a crescendo that may fizzle-fail-flatten
in a pileup of electricity
and heartsick thunderheads cracking open.

But if humidity holds into the night
there will be a quiet shift
when the darkened air cools
to the catalyst moment of dew.

A sudden coagulation
vapor to droplet, out of suspension.
At once, everything gathered falls into place.
And you will likely miss it.

I'm Still Last

In our first few months,
you often came
with a baby
who sang
under our conversations
simple sounds from her newly made body.

As a nanny,
you looked just like someone's young wife.
You have so much to give, I told you
in my first attempt
to miss this.
I'm just not ready to receive it.

Later, elsewhere
I'm still last
to recognize the sweet edges of what's next.

We Kiss

We kiss soft and elegant like snails,
climbing upside down, slicked
from the surface by shine.
That wetness keeps space for us too
keeps our friction down, keeps us
from getting stuck...Crepuscular—
our libido comes out in the in-betweens.

Except for that Saturday at noon
when you saw me in the mirror
and took the shirt from my hands,
or last week when the moon shone
so bright at 4 a.m. that we couldn't sleep.
What else to do?

Villanelle for When We End

Don't ever think it didn't matter,
when, just for a moment, I opened.
Plainly said, I needed a kind of love.

Not that field-razing, earth-baking blaze
but a gentle, generous thing that didn't pretend.
Don't ever think it didn't matter.

I keep buried a smooth stone all mine,
even when it doesn't feel like an end.
Plainly said, I needed the kind of love

with letters and too-long looks, affection
that waited like eddies and overflowed.
Don't ever think it didn't matter.

Like that gray autumn rain, you poured
a warm drink long overdue. I gardened.
Plainly said, I needed your kind of love.

And you needed mine: a slow, heavy soil that
set bounds from which we made our upward wend.
Don't ever think it didn't matter.
Plainly said, we needed that kind of love.

Each Blessing

In the quiet still of morning,
things are just beginning
or continuing.
The sun warms the world
and it is easier
to feel each blessing
of windows and fresh air
of dew and light
of pluffed pillows on the couch
of green garlic
chopped for breakfast omelets
and the clamorous shelves of books
still waiting to be read
and the rested feel of my skin
and my spreading toes.

Holy

When we twist in bed
stripped and panting
your eyes sing
hymns.

I place your name
next to God's
in my mouth
punctuate the two with

oh—Oh—

My Woman

Pink-breasted from sun
my woman can lap the lake
or listen all day.

Morgan's First Hat

It is warm. It fits but
here the pattern shifts
for half a gray-green row.
Here two stitches dropped
leave a small hole.
Here some looseness pulls
along the edge.

I wear them happily, the patterns
of your practice.
All the while, you lost count
tangled the yarn hopelessly
and spent hours frowning, laughing
carefully pulling the raw strands apart
to try again.

You won't make them again,
these precious mistakes.

Extra Butter

You taught my belly to soften.
The tight band of sexy unbuckled
and the word wandered.

Sexy became always
buying extra butter
letting mealtimes linger.

With subtle progression
from thin to fertile
body became a thing to feel.

An animated world
beneath skin and muscle
where organs squeeze and wrestle.

Where they work their messy work
to keep this body energized.
Why not be mesmerized?

The Days You Bother Me

The days you bother me
I know you must be
more deeply
family.

The Deep Settle

Winter Solstice 2022

The story of lovers is
insistent
so when I look at my hands
on my woman's face
they seem like a man's.
Also when those hands
chop wood, take apart the car
drill together the bed frame.

Our story opens
in a sideways kind of bloom.
Conversations of union roll over
our skies like new constellations.
Who asks who?
Our steps unguided
unmapped.

Nights with you, the dark ripples
like linen sheets bare with
promise
and patience.
"Whenever you're ready,"
you say. The stars

aren't going anywhere.

Again the sun is setting.
The bony trees let in
more of the quilted light above.
Come walk with me
in the shadowed woods along the path
we know so well. Today,
it's different.

A loop of precious beads
—a stand-in for Elsie's heirloom ring—
waits on the flat riverstone
glinting in the last light of the shortest day.

"Will you?"
Less question, more invitation.
The days just get longer from here.

Early Talks with Our Sperm Donor

A certain sensuality shimmers
in his kindness.
In the simple shared meals
and long talks
there's a charge
something vital moving
wanting shape
feeling wanted.
There's a closeness
in holding out this tender desire
in asking for help.
We can't help but trust
his smile—and begin to
unknowingly conspire.

Falling in Love Together

Here, you are my sister
giddy and glowing
squealing at the details
recounting each word, each touch.
"And then what?"

Then, we are lovers
reinvigorated.
The known places of skin
freshened by a tough trust
and just a touch of jealousy.

Sharing you, I see again
why I fell in love with you
and your sparkling many smiles
while we fall-fall-splash.

At the bottom, clear water
catches us and we're back
in the Yucatan cenotes
gliding under trailing roots, inside
a buried coconut of sweet water.

How Can This Be?

"How can this be?
But it is."
—Mary Oliver

These hands touching, holding
full of heat and sweet.
The wholeness of our harmonies
cooked my heart until it slumped
in its own syrup like strawberries.

Yet melancholy lingered
threatening rot.
How could it not?
Who gets it this good?

But here we are, feeding
a dream we hope is hot enough
to raze the quick-growing competition
and leave the long oaks
room to thicken their slow bark
and grow something lasting.

Attempt #1

Take my hand
and feel
the bellied longing.

I know no one
is everything.
But I don't see the walls yet.

Total faith.
Isn't that what it takes?

Fecundity

Our bare skin slips under
the reflecting skin of water
on the warm pond
and the smell of sex melts
into the smell of mud and reeds.
The frogs croak from the soft shore.
The moon and stars make
a world of silhouettes.

Lights, chorus, all this material
mating
to make more, more.
It has little to do with me.
It's life
here in the pond.

In day or dark
the world wants to multiply—
the mosquito, the bullfrog, the firefly.
We too conduct that electric persistence
to go on.
Beneath our careful, creative complications,
just this—
I want a son.

II.

Love in Practice

Spring

Heed the early spring
when the hasty pears jump
their buds and blacken
in the next week's frost.
Even trees get their timing wrong.
Don't take it to heart.
Always, next year offers its empty pages.
And anyways, the plums flowered perfectly.

Alone for the Night

I sent a letter in her hands
to give to the man we love.

Permissive words to say
touch her, love her, enjoy each other.

I wait for jealousy or some cousin
to stroll through this empty house.

But just the cat pads across the clean floors
and a solemn echo of someone else's joy.

"I Heard You Got Married"

It's easy to forget.
Three months past our ceremony,
I barely notice my ring
until it scrapes against the bathtub.

My wife is out,
and my attention has drifted
from the tinny voice reading
through the phone speaker.

The water is warm,
my hair, half wet.
I'm almost lonely.
Then, the water-muted scratch.

Before we ascended the altar, we took a walk.
A slow path down from the barn
where long tables displayed flowers
and bright, mismatched napkins.

We passed the garden
in its late summer grandeur.
Squash vines crowded close and low,
and corn shook tired tassels at the sky.

And the two of us walked
just like any other day
except for long dresses and mascaraed lashes
and the photographer hovering behind us.

But no one was around to tell us
Hurry up!
We had time.
We have time.

The great promise of marriage is this:
I will spend my time with you.
I give you my time.
It is all we have to give, really.

It is so easy to forget
amid the emails, grocery lists, taking out the trash,
packing lunches, washing dishes, driving here,
    driving there—
But look!

As we merge onto the highway in the early winter
    dark,
a star
races down the sky, vanishing
just before it crosses the dash.

"What does that mean?" she asks.
And to my unexpected relief, I don't need it to
mean anything.
I don't need to solve
whatever big question we are hunting tonight.

I don't need to know *right*
or *best* or *when* or *how.*
I am not alone,
and we are together now.

Rhythm Villanelle

There is a rhythm to the days
that banters between my body and yours.
We move like dancers.

Sleep and wake, eat and empty, connect and break.
We will never stay the same, but
there is a rhythm to the days.

Even when I am away,
my travel is braided with your sounds, smells.
We move like dancers.

It's not performance, but it's warming to watch.
The same words, repeated, mean more.
There is a rhythm to the days.

It evolves in tempo and layers.
Our feet find new steps, crossing among the old.
We move like dancers.

The mornings and endings carry on.
Beside mine, your body carries on.
There is a rhythm to the days.
We move like dancers.

Love in Practice

We sit across the kitchen
in red rocking chair and yellow stool
and take the other's perspective.
Nothing poisonous withstands
the tender way she sees me.
The struggle lightens at last, bubbling
up from the tight underground and rises
like a day I can simply experience.
She calls back my gentleness
hiding from the voices that spit
"What's wrong with me? Why can't I just…?"
When forgiveness crawls from the earth
she rubs in the dirt like vernix.

How Much Do You Love Me?

"How much do you love me?"
A big, heavy ocean.
"Water is heavy. Can you love me light too?"
Yes, like clouds on the wind.

Nightmares

In the crescent night
I wake in the middle of your sentence
...bad dreams...
like a plea for something different
I roll over
your troubled face gray in the moonlight
tucks like a mammal
under my chin
I fold you in close
shh shh it's okay
I think I say
sleep still heavy and blurring and dark
but from somewhere the sweetness
comes forth certain that this
is important
to hug and hold
and make some soft noise
I can't follow you
into dreams
we lie out here
in the vast sheets together
and hope
the sun rises orange like
yesterday and the day before
and hope

we can still trust something
we were told was true
if only that a body can comfort
and dreams are only dreams

Attempt #2

Mistakes in hand
feel and try
again. Slower, this time.

I know we need
to let go
of those iceberg expectations.

Doesn't every story
have at least one close call?

Why Do You Meditate with Your Eyes Open?

To see where the colors go
and the songs, he says.

See, the sky is everywhere
in the space between
the trees and clouds
where the winged ones course through.
It is easier to see there, above,
than in the space between
my fingers or my teeth
where doing and saying
are always trafficking by.

All material is dissolved into sky
and the skies between cells.
Every magnificent space
behind a thriving clutter.

Instead of Missing You

A constant breeze kept me company
for the week.
The ceiling fans spun in every room.

Without you to listen to
I heard the rain.
And the crack of the tallest branch of the peach tree.
Nearly all the fruits
now blush orange and reach
for the soil, sweet towards sweet.

Without you listening to me
words turned from throat down other roads
walking the curve of my skull
vague pilgrims
moving as sensation through skin.
Thoughts looped, complicated
and exited as sigh or shiver.

I sat through the day and tried to notice.

Do Not Forget to Subtract

Do not forget to subtract
in this ever-lengthening, ever-complicating life.
Always, the neon signs shout "MORE!"
but do not forget about less.

Two Ways to Change

Dress for wind—
wrap your coat tight
and go stone-like.
Press your back
to the insistent force.
Dig your lonely strength
and grip the grasses.
Don't let it slip away,
all you've gained and prayed for
everything that's *yours*.
Pull in every loose strand.
Let everything outside change.

Open your kite wings to the whipping gale.
Let it tear buttons, loose hairs
like it could lift you, trembling, skywards
to whisk you somewhere blue.
Spread your hands and let it pass through.
How could anyone hold on?
Even the names of things vanish, even songs
flip their rhythms and trade language.
Turn out your pockets and grow clearer,
emptier, closer to the wind.
Let it all change.

When the gusts finally still,
the ground will be beneath
still wet and warming
and still full.

Honeymoon on the Coast of Maine

On a rock at the edge of the sea
with just bare feet beneath me, I watch how
the water patterns the sand, the wind patterns the
water,
my wife holds my hand.
As we walk back down the beach
our words scuttle and pause and float
like the gulls playing on the rough wind.
The conversation of two who don't need to talk
but want the other to know
I am with you, I am thinking of us.
And the us opens freely
as the wind blowing sand across sand
and we send our love up on the
bent wings of seagulls
to a man many winds away
driving home, thinking of us.

Fantasizing

I spent the hour
before dawn
loving you

my mind
body
imagining

my
climax
your own.

Doubt

This panic
carries me careless
and lost in love
across a field of grasses
sick with cicadas
who—riled and yellow with rage—
are lost too.

I find the creek,
toss my body among the rocks
and build a riverstone roof
live with the salamanders
hidden and soft and ask
over and over
What *isn't* a gift?

When I find my hands again
I catch a water spider
the flailing strider rifted
from its mystical walk on tension.

If I swallow it,
can I, too, balance?
walk on water?
slide on the surface?

never sink?
never drown?
never be heavy
again?

Attempt #3

I have no hand
in this
anymore.

We are trying again
and I don't know how
we will do it.

But I pray now.

Take Your Time

Even if everything
is dragging you
towards the fateful fork—
Wait.

Wait, until you feel the answer seep up
well-cold and spring-clear.
Wait. It must not be time yet
if you don't have an answer.

The answer is not knowing (necessarily)
but a breeze moving through the pines
whose branches break as they grow
whose tips sway tall above.

Take your time,
a day
is just a day.
An end, an end.

I'm Almost Done

I'm almost done
chasing an ideal
waiting
for something I don't entirely want.
Unreasonable.
Whatever reason is.
It seems to change
but slower these days.

The dances
more and more
are only dances.
The music ends
and everyone goes home
washes off each other's fragrance.

Turns out
both creeks led back
to the same waterway
and I'm not
so rebellious after all.

I hope that you find
what you are looking for
and that I do, too,

and that we keep
running together sometimes
like little waterfalls
pouring off the same stone.

Imposter

Every boat is far ahead
sails crisp and full of wind
while I
rig patchwork cloth
twist and tilt
and roll along in the salting
uncatchable breeze that always seems
to be changing direction.

But I continue tying
these knots and walking across
the pitching deck.
Every day, I wake on the water
sailing all the same.

I Haven't Caught the Answer Yet

So I am wading in the dark water
feeling the slick-bodied future
swim around my legs,
so cool and edgeless
it could just be
a strong current
water moving water.
But then—
it brushes
against my skin.
The weight and form are there
then, gone.

III.

What Matters

Attempt #4

It's too late now
but somewhere else
or some other time
or to a few someones
who are almost us
but not quite,
it's happening another way.
Our dreams are weaving
the threads of ideal and possible
into a woven plane of real.

And in that other somewhere
or other time
or with those other someones
different things are harder
and others are smoother
and the conversations
have almost the same lines
but are colored in yellow, pink, green
instead of black and blue and silver.

It Is About the Walk

Of course it was
naïve.
Every love
is a farther trek than it appears.
Good thing.
How many lessons are learned
journeying to a dead end?
Or journeying back?

You are no bird
coasting high above the map
but a long-footed lover
crashing
through the thickets.

Connection, Rupture, Repair

I thought one day we would reach it.
The finish line of the final form.
And it would feel inevitable
once we were there
like it was always meant
to settle where it did.
And there we would tread water
in some picturesque pond
with no more journeying required.
The dragonflies would come and go.
The tadpoles would grow up and leg away.
And we would watch, reminiscing
inside a peaceful, static fate.

But oh, that is so not where it goes.
Even ponds dry up and refill
on rainwater or spring seep.
This thing between us is alive
a process, not an arrival.
A constant cycle from
connection to rupture to repair.

The moments, the synchronicities
our hands clasped and swinging
between our walks, our eyes locked

our words making sense
to each other, days aligning
the pattern pulling us along.

Until
it changes. And not
for the better.
Mistake. Crack.
Forgotten favor. Crack.
I don't understand. Crack.
I miss you. Crack.
This isn't working. Crack.
Flat tire. Split shoe. Wrong turn.
Crack. I lost the pattern.
Limping and lurching and late.

Until we slow
maybe turn back or just sit
to catch a breath.
Reset, quiet down, apologize
and find some way to laugh
and ask—"Can I try again?"
and again? and again? and
we're back again
to the pulling pattern of connection.

Gone

Far sudden and vast
the quiet side of the bed
where I knew your breath.

Simon

He has the kind of smell
that is just himself.
Sometimes woodsmoke
or lamb and buttered onions
but mostly
the wax of life rubbing off his skin
like an animal
clean and itself
without trying.

I'm still
sleeping in his
white cotton T-shirt
that doesn't even smell like him
anymore.
Entertaining unhinged dreams
set off by
the deafening inner roar
of airplane-turbulence prayers
"I don't want to—
Not now—
Not without—"

She thinks she's crazy
titrating off the heroin love

that is nothing like that
but caring and honest
and again wanting what
we can't have because
we didn't choose it—or couldn't do it—
how many times?

The grief keeps
crushing the fruits
of whatever else we grow.
But I think
the wine will be delicious
years from now
when we've forgotten the mess
of juice and bottles and stains
when, finally, we're old friends
(who probably still want to fuck)
laughing at every
logical attempt
to figure out loving or living.

Until then, I am loving you
—at my best—
like an animal
loves
clean and itself
without wondering.

The Whippoorwill

The whippoorwill says
nothing new,
just the same looping phrase
and again and again and again.
It doesn't bore me.
Every warm evening he is out
whistling his rhythmic tune at 9 o'clock.
A reminder. You do not always need
to be recreating yourself.
If you find your tune,
sing it.
Sing again and again and again.

Another New House

The dawn is blue on this side of the clouds.
The boxes are finally broken down.

Here again is the bed frame
a cutting board, a spoon.

Pieces you cut and carved, left behind
that keen aesthetic eye.

You know it can't be rushed
the making of a good, lasting thing.

An eighth of an inch
will make the difference.

Whether the pieces fit
or not...

I still reach for you, always guessing
too hasty to measure.

Are your hands
making something new?

What Is in Your Heart?

What is in your heart?
How will it get out?

More than—force
there is
every exit
which keeps us moving.
The back door
rolling open.

"I walk," says the woman
who lost her son.
"Every day. Far."

What Matters

What matters is the weight.
Your body
pressed against a friend who shakes.
Or the basket of your arms
holding the flopping weight
of someone else's babe.
Every fierce embrace
that holds together the grieving.
The fast hand that steadies
or slows a fall.
The way we all
hold one another.

Crying Resolves

The shaking world throws off
anything pent up.
So the trees shed twigs and leaves
and the rabbit shudders post-chase
and you leak seawater
even though you long left the waves.

I Dropped the Ball

"I dropped the ball."
Yes, I dropped one too—yesterday.
Off it rolled
down whatever gentle slope
until some open hand lifted it up again
or it found a storm drain
and floated until it met the ocean.

Where the Crawdad Walks

It is okay
to feel success is elsewhere and quieter.
Whatever current of this wide river
catches your heart
it is flowing towards something greater.
The white rapids and shallow ripples
all carry the same water.
It's okay to want
the slow, clear eddy
where the crawdad
walks across the settled silt.
Someone else will flip the kayaks
and love it.

At the Window

The doors shut.

No to this version.
No to that one too.
No wish can keep them open.

Goodbye.
Goodbye.

But at the window,
knocking.

Remember This

A marriage blessing composed of excerpts from letters and speeches my wife and I received at our wedding in September of 2023.

The big day is only the beginning
of the world you will be building together.
Love can change the world. It will change you.
There is nothing to fear.
You have more strength than you know.

Remember this—or imagine—
You were (and are) fearless
        in your love—like hawks
        lock feet and dance-fall in spectacular
        spirals of attraction—this is how
I imagine your souls.
Unafraid to be honest,
you reinforce each other.

Remember this—
You will not always agree.
Being right is not as important
        as being together.
You've created a life together.
This is a miracle.

In heated moments
take a walk
remember to lean on each other
ask for closeness
find balance
laugh, always laugh.

You two are complementary beings.
May you drop your mirrors
and turn toward each other.
Contrast can create abiding—integral—
harmonies, so
reach for others.

You both brought me back to earth.
Thank the sweet waters
that you are in my life.
I see you as the thread that binds and weaves.
Please call on me if you have lost the threads.

In conclusion, Love. Love. Love.
Remember—
this is a miracle.

Acknowledgments

The act of writing is often solitary, even lonely, but the drive to create is a response to all the varied connections I make with those around me.

So, thank you to all the relationships that put the juice in my days. Thank you to the mountains who are always there to listen and to the streams and rivers that wake me up and loosen what is stuck. Thank you to my teachers who kept me digging and discovering, and who taught me to appreciate the editing process.

Thank you to the team at Otterpine for making this book a reality, walking me through the many steps of publishing, and listening to my vision.

Thank you to my family for your love and support, particularly my mother who has been cheering on my love of writing since I was a child. Thank you, Megan, for unknowingly giving me the title of this book. Thank you, Jake, for challenging me and inspiring me and always asking what I'm writing.

Thank you, Simon, for everything.

Thank you, Morgan, always.

With Gratitude

I am deeply grateful to the people who contributed financially to help bring this book to print. Thank you for believing in the value of my work and making it possible for these poems to find their way onto the page and out into the hands and hearts of readers.

Susie Bell
Beth Berry
Susan Denne
Sandy Dickie
Brianna Gorham
Todd Gorham
Oliver Hassell
Benjamin Haynes
Annie Heath

Wells Hill
Amanda Holden
Kristy Johnson
Stefan Kelischek
Nichols Mabry
Jeremy Migner
Martha Nelson
Mary Constance Commagere Roth
Maggie Schlubach
Kathy Sheppard
Mary Morgaine Squire
Joan Walker

About the Author

Lucille May lives with her wife outside Asheville, North Carolina, where she works on local farms, tends a vibrant home, writes poems and creative nonfiction, and practices living a connected, embodied life. Lucille began writing as a child and never stopped. She studied Creative Writing at UNC Asheville and is drawn to subjects including relationships, food and farming, birth and death, and the spirituality inherent in our physical world. *Thank the Sweet Waters* is Lucille's first poetry collection.

www.ingramcontent.com/pod-product-compliance
Lightning Source LLC
Chambersburg PA
CBHW020800130626
46554CB00006B/2288